Making Headway
Intermediate

Talking in Pairs

Tania Bastow
Ceri Jones

Oxford University Press

Oxford University Press
Walton Street, Oxford OX2 6DP

Oxford New York
Athens Auckland Bangkok Bombay
Calcutta Cape Town Dar es Salaam Delhi
Florence Hong Kong Istanbul Karachi
Kuala Lumpur Madras Madrid Melbourne
Mexico City Nairobi Paris Singapore
Taipei Tokyo Toronto

and associated companies in
Berlin Ibadan

OXFORD and OXFORD ENGLISH are trade marks of
Oxford University Press

ISBN 0 19 435555 1

Typeset by Wyvern Typesetting Ltd, Bristol
Printed in Hong Kong

Acknowledgements

The authors would like to thank their paren
and the following for all their help and
support:
John and Liz Soars
Marion and Mark Irvine
Patricia Di Risio
Jo Malcolm
All the students at the English School of
L'Aquila
Carla Cardinale

Illustrations by
Brett Breckon
Gordon Hendry
Matthew Lawrence
Vanessa Luff
Sharon Pallent
Colin Salmon
Tim Slade
Margaret Wellbank

Location photography by
Emily Anderson
Paul Freestone

The publishers and authors would like to
thank the following for their kind permissi
to reproduce photographs:
Barnaby's Picture Library
The Anthony Blake Picture Library
James Davis Travel Photography
Ecoscene
The Hulton Deutsch Collection Ltd
Kos Picture Source Ltd
Popperfoto
Still Pictures Environmental Agency

ntents

Foreword

Talking in Pairs

The interdependent skills of listening and speaking are probably the one given most prominence in the modern language classroom. Learners of English want to be able to use the language in a wide range of situation and for whatever purposes they might need it. Teachers are therefore constantly looking for material which will either practise discrete language areas (for example, the Present simple, or prepositions), or wi provide the opportunity for some free speaking practice for its own sake where students use whatever language they have at their disposal. *Talking in Pairs* contains material that fulfils both of these objectives.

Most of the activities are based on the information gap principle, that i both Student A and Student B have similar tasks, but they have differe information. They need to discuss and negotiate to complete the activit These so-called communication games require students to react to wha they hear and to respond spontaneously and appropriately as a result. The interactions are thus not mechanical, but meaningful.

The authors of *Talking in Pairs* have selected extremely lively topics, soi familiar, some refreshingly new to ELT. They have also created relevan stimulating material to accompany them. We feel sure that teachers w want to dip into the book for supplementary activities as and when the consider it necessary, and that they will also be able to rely on *Talking Pairs* to provide a complete listening and speaking-based lesson if they need it. Equally, we feel sure that students will be motivated to explore the topics, that they will be challenged by the tasks and, very importantly, that they will have a lot of fun doing them.

John and Liz Soars
Series editors

Introduction

this book is for

This book is for students using *Headway Intermediate* or any other coursebook at a similar level, who want additional practice in the speaking skills they have learnt. It is primarily a pairwork book designed to get students communicating in ways that are interesting and challenging to the imagination.

the book is nized

The book is designed to be dipped into, and the units can therefore be used independently of each other. Each unit takes approximately forty-five minutes to one hour of class time. A unit consists of a **Warmer** and a **Speaking** activity, sometimes supplemented by a **Listening** activity.

to use the book

The activities in the book are self-explanatory. However, here are a few general hints to help you, the teacher.

1 As it is important to focus the students' attention on the topic from the start, it is not advisable to omit the **Warmer**. This first section also provides an opportunity to preview much of the vocabulary in the rest of the unit.

2 Try to keep a low profile during the **Speaking** activities. It is best to allow students to speak freely, even if they make mistakes, as this gives them confidence in expressing themselves.

3 Some pages carry an instruction to cover the opposite page. In units 5, 7, 10 and 11, for example, it is vitally important to draw the students' attention to the instructions before going on, and to make sure that they follow them at all times. Otherwise, the information gap element is lost.

A sample teacher's guide to Unit 1

Warmer (page 7)

1 Check that the students understand the instructions and any new language before they start the exercise. You may want to give the a short period of silence to read through the exercise and ask questions. Once the students start, it is important to let them do th activity with minimum input from you. A multilingual class studyi away from home can talk about the town they are studying in.

2 When the students have finished, bring the class back together aga to compare and discuss their answers. If there are any doubts or disagreements, the students should be encouraged to discuss them class.

Speaking (pages 8–11)

1 Make sure the students understand their roles in the activity and emphasize the importance of not letting their partners see their pa; Let the students prepare silently for a short period before they star Once they have started, keep a low profile and let them get on witl the activity, helping only if really necessary.

2 When the students have finished, bring the class together again. A each pair to present their programme for the visitors, then discuss which they think is the most appropriate. This is a good time to gi the class feedback on any language problems.

Listening (page 12)

Not all the units have a listening section. In this unit, it is an extra activity which can be used after the speaking activity to consolidate t discussion in the feedback stage.

1 Twin towns

mer

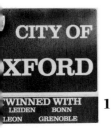

> **,twin 'town** either of a pair of towns, usually in different countries, that have established special links with each other: *Oxford and Bonn are twin towns.* ○ *Oxford's twin town in France is Grenoble.*

1 Work in pairs. Write down two places in your town under each heading below.

Typical places to visit	**Factories, businesses**
_____	_____
_____	_____
Restaurants	**Schools, colleges, universities**
_____	_____
_____	_____
Sports facilities	**Places you would never take a tourist**
_____	_____
_____	_____

2 Now compare your answers with other students in the class.

Student A Turn to pages 8–9.
Student B Turn to pages 10–11.

Speaking

Student A

You and your partner are members of a committee responsible for twinning your town. You want to twin your town with a small town England called Budleigh Salterton. So you have invited four people from Budleigh Salterton to visit your town.

1 Read the information about two of your guests, and fill in the form opposite.

CURRICULUM VITAE

Name:	Simon Davenport
Address:	19 Heather Lane,
	Budleigh Salterton,
	EX9 6AF
Telephone:	0395 435664
Marital status:	Single
Age:	31

Education and qualifications

BSc Engineering, Exeter University
PhD in telecommunications, Oxford University

Work experience

John Brown Engineering Group (two years)
IBM London (one year)
Budleigh Salterton Civil Engineering Department (at present)

Hobbies and leisure-time activities

Windsurfing, skiing, walking, stamp collecting and reading

I work very closely with Budleigh Salterton's Emergency Services and would appreciate the opportunity of finding out more about how your police, fire, and ambulance emergency services function.

I would also like to visit any sports centres in your town. Perhaps next year we could organize a football, volleyball, or tennis match between our towns?

Yours sincerely

Simon Davenport

PS I'm afraid I don't like sightseeing very much. Would it be possible for me to do some of the things above instead?

Catherine Smith
25 Bay Road
Budleigh Salterton
EX9 2AD
20 May

Dear Organizer
Thank you for your invitation to visit your town. I'm really looking forward to my trip.

I work at home, as I am married with two small children. I make sweets and desserts for restaurants in the area. I would be interested in visiting local restaurants and picking up some traditional recipes, as well as meeting other self-employed people. I'd also like to visit your Town Hall.

I'd love to do some sightseeing - but no museums, please! I find

Budleigh Salterton is a small town on the south coast of England. It is next to the sea, and is famous as the birthplace of Sir Walter Raleigh.

Name	Age	Interests	Other information

2 Now ask your partner about the other two visitors. Answer your partner's questions and fill in the rest of the form.

3 Then, with your partner, plan two exciting and informative days for the visitors to your town. Try to keep the group together as much as possible, but also try to keep everyone happy. When you are planning their itinerary, remember to include travel time, means of transport, etc.

Time	Day 1	Day 2
Coffee break		
Lunch		
Tea break		
Dinner and evening		

Speaking

Student B

You and your partner are members of a committee responsible for twinning your town. You want to twin your town with a small town England called Budleigh Salterton. So you have invited four people fro Budleigh Salterton to visit your town.

1 Read the information about two of your guests, and fill in the form opposite.

LUCKY JENNY

Eighteen-year-old Jenny Wong has won our 'Cultural Exchange' competition for answering ten questions on different cultures in the most understanding and original way. And she'll soon be flying out to our twin town for a two-day trip. When asked what she hoped to learn in the two days, Jenny replied, 'I want to meet the people, especially people of my age to see whether we're different or just the same. I'd like to look around some of their schools and colleges, clubs, discos – you know – places where people hang out. And of course I want to do all the touristy things people do!' Well, enjoy yourself Jenny and let us know how you got on when you get back.

21 Exmouth Road
Budleigh Salterton
EX9 3BA
23 May

Dear Organizer

My name is Peter Grundy and I shall be joining the group visiting your town next month.

First, a little information about myself. I am a retired historian and I write history books. I love travelling, and I am looking forward to meeting the people, seeing some of the countryside, and exploring your town - the old and the new parts!

There is one small problem I should tell you about: I can't walk for too long because of my rheumatism.

Budleigh Salterton is a small town on the south coast of England. It is next to the sea, and is famous as the birthplace of Sir Walter Raleigh.

Name	Age	Interests	Other information

2   Now answer your partner's questions. Then ask about the other two visitors and fill in the rest of the form.

3   Then, with your partner, plan two exciting and informative days for the visitors to your town. Try to keep the group together as much as possible, but also try to keep everyone happy. When you are planning their itinerary, remember to include travel time, means of transport, etc.

Time	Day 1	Day 2
Coffee break		
Lunch		
Tea break		
Dinner and evening		

Listening

The four guests from Budleigh Salterton have now returned from their visit and are being interviewed on the local radio.

1   Work in pairs. Before you listen, try to imagine which parts of your pla they enjoyed most.

T.1

2   Now listen to the four visitors talking about their trip. Then fill in the grid below.

Name	Best part of the trip

2 What a night!

Work in pairs and look at the six pictures below. They all belong to the same story. What do you think it's about?

Student A Turn to pages 14–15.
Student B Turn to pages 16–17.

Speaking

Student A

1   Look at the four pictures. They are part of a story. There are eight pictures altogether. Your partner has the other four pictures. Describe your pictures to your partner and listen to his/her descriptions. Togeth put the pictures in the right order and write the correct number in the boxes, without looking at each other's pages.

2 When you have finished, look at your partner's pictures. Help each other to retell the story in the right order.

Speaking

Student B

1 Look at the four pictures. They are part of a story. There are eight pictures altogether. Your partner has the other four pictures. Listen to your partner describing his/her pictures. Then describe yours. Together put the pictures in the right order and write the correct number in the boxes, without looking at each other's pages.

g.

h.

2 When you have finished, look at your partner's pictures. Help each other to retell the story in the right order.

Listening

1   Which picture or pictures would you choose to finish the story? Why?

T.2

2   Now listen to a radio news story about the break-in. Which of the situations in the pictures are mentioned? Tick (√) the items.

3 The English teacher

1 With your partner, discuss the questions on the board in the picture.

The English lesson

- Have you ever taught someone to do something? If so, what?

- Would you like to be a teacher? If yes, what would you like to teach? If no, why not?

2 If you were teaching English as a foreign language to beginners, in what order would you teach the language items below? Put them in order of priority from 1–6.

☐ Numbers (*1–100–1,000*)
☐ The alphabet (*A, B, C/How do you spell ...?*)
☐ Personal questions (*What's your name/age/nationality?*)
☐ *Can* (*Can you play tennis?*)
☐ The present simple (*Do you like ...? I like/I don't like ...*)
☐ The time (*What's the time?*)

3 Now compare your order with the others in the class. Is there anything else you would like to teach a beginner?

Speaking

Students A and B

You work in a secondary school. The English teacher has broken her l[e]
and will not be able to come to work for at least three weeks. You and
your partner are the only teachers who speak English, so the Headteac[her]
has asked you to teach the English lessons. You cannot say no!

The students in your class are 14–16 year-old beginners. They started [a]
month ago, and have had two hours of English a week.

1 Look at the information below. Work together with your partner to fin[d]
out what the students have studied so far. Use the space below to mak[e]
notes.

English

Lesson 1

Name? Where from?
Number 1-10

Lesson 2

Revise: Name? Where from?
Teach: Age? Nationality?
　　　Numbers 10-100

---

1 March Homework

1 It's seven o'clock. ✔
2 It's twenty-five past seven. ✔
3 It's seven past quarter. ✗
4 It's half past two. ✔
5 It's

Week 3

Teach: verb 'to be' and expressions:
How do you say x in English?
I'm sorry, I don't understand etc.

---

12 March Homework

1 This is a map. ✔
2 That are a book. ✗
3 Those is windows. ✗
4 These are tables. ✔
5 This is my bo[ok]

Vocabulary list

1 good　　6 thirsty
2 bad　　7 hungry
3 clever　8 old
　　　　9 young

Week 4

Teach: Would you like something to
eat/drink?
+ food and drink vocabulary

Lesson plans - week 2

Revise personal pronouns
Teach: What's her name?
　　What's his name? etc.

A map of the school

| Library |
| Your Room |
Computer Room	Science
	Science
	Science

This is a map of the school[.]
You are here, next to th[e]
library. The computer roo[m]
is here, opposite th[e]
science labs. The classroom[s]
are on both sides of th[e]
corridor. At the end of th[e]
corridor there is a door t[o]
the playground and garden[.]

Language studied so far:

2 Now discuss with your partner what you would like to teach or revise in the next three weeks.

	WEEK 1	WEEK 2	WEEK 3
T U E S D A Y			
T H U R S D A Y			

3 Finally, decide how you are going to teach your first lesson. Discuss your ideas with your partner.

New language to teach :

Warmer (short, fun activity to start the lesson) :

First exercise :

Second exercise :

Homework :

4 Up in space

1 Discuss which of these things you prefer and why.
1 A circle or a square
2 Playing tennis or working out in a gym
3 A jacuzzi or a sauna
4 An aquarium or green plants
5 A bus or a taxi (when you travel)
6 A good book or good company (on a long journey)

2 Did any of your partner's answers surprise you? Do you think you and your partner would enjoy travelling together?

Speaking 1

It is the 23rd century. Global warming has resulted in dangerously high sea levels, covering an extra ten per cent of the world's land mass. The world's governments are encouraging mass emigration to space, where a man-made space station, Cerinia 1000, is waiting to host 200,000,000 new space inhabitants. You and your partner have applied for space emigration and you are looking at spaceships available on the market. For financial reasons you have decided to buy a spaceship together.

1 Before you start planning, read the government regulations and find out how many passengers you must have on your spaceship.

SPACE POOLS REGULATIONS

The following regulations must be followed by all space immigrants travelling in private spaceships.

1 All spaceships must carry a minimum of four passengers for maximum energy efficiency.

2 All spaceships must carry at least two women aged between 20 and 40.

3 All spaceships must carry at least one man aged between 20 and 50.

4 All spaceships must carry at least two members of the following list of professions:

DOCTOR NURSE CIVIL ENGINEER ELECTRONIC ENGINEER
ELECTRICIAN PLUMBER FARMER VET BOTANIST

If the passenger list does not include the above-mentioned passengers, the private spaceship will be forced to accept guests chosen by the government, or lift-off will not be permitted.

---

2 Discuss with your partner who you would like to take with you, and why.

Student A Turn to pages 24–5.
Student B Turn to pages 26–7.

Speaking 2

Student A

On these pages you have some information about the space capsules available.

1 With your partner, decide what your priorities are, and use the form below to make notes. You have £10,000,000 to spend, but remember, you can also make your other passengers pay!

The Pyramid	The Bus	The Cube	The Sphere

2 Now ask your partner for any other information you would like on the space capsules. When you have all the information you need, decide wit your partner which space capsule is best for you.

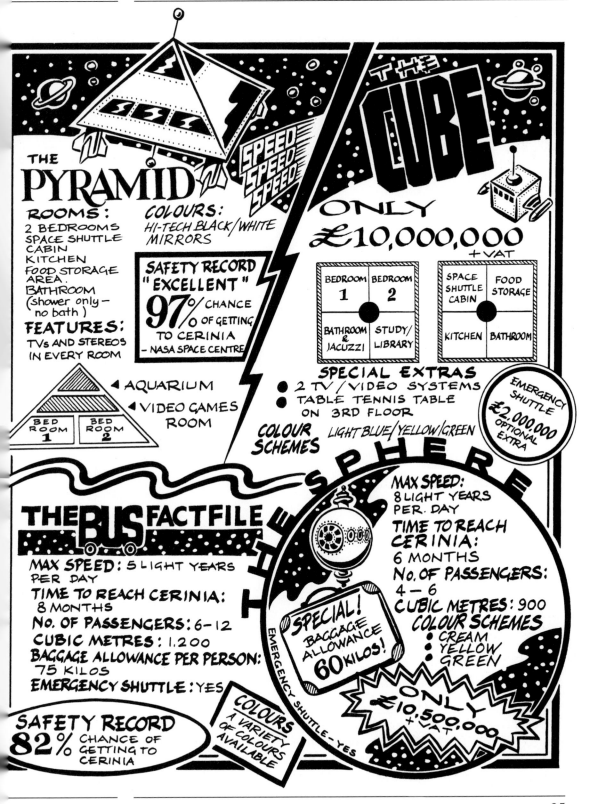

THE PYRAMID

ROOMS:
2 BEDROOMS
SPACE SHUTTLE CABIN
KITCHEN
FOOD STORAGE AREA.
BATHROOM (shower only – no bath)

FEATURES:
TVs AND STEREOS IN EVERY ROOM

COLOURS:
HI-TECH BLACK/WHITE MIRRORS

SAFETY RECORD "EXCELLENT"
97% CHANCE OF GETTING TO CERINIA
– NASA SPACE CENTRE

◀ AQUARIUM
◀ VIDEO GAMES ROOM

BED ROOM 1   BED ROOM 2

SPEED SPEED SPEED

THE CUBE

ONLY **£10,000,000** + VAT

| BEDROOM 1 | BEDROOM 2 |
| BATHROOM & JACUZZI | STUDY/LIBRARY |

| SPACE SHUTTLE CABIN | FOOD STORAGE |
| KITCHEN | BATHROOM |

SPECIAL EXTRAS
• 2 TV/VIDEO SYSTEMS
• TABLE TENNIS TABLE ON 3RD FLOOR

COLOUR SCHEMES LIGHT BLUE/YELLOW/GREEN

EMERGENCY SHUTTLE **£2,000,000** OPTIONAL EXTRA

THE BUS FACTFILE

MAX SPEED: 5 LIGHT YEARS PER DAY
TIME TO REACH CERINIA: 8 MONTHS
No. OF PASSENGERS: 6–12
CUBIC METRES: 1,200
BAGGAGE ALLOWANCE PER PERSON: 75 KILOS
EMERGENCY SHUTTLE: YES

SAFETY RECORD
82% CHANCE OF GETTING TO CERINIA

COLOURS A VARIETY OF COLOURS AVAILABLE

THE SPHERE

MAX SPEED: 8 LIGHT YEARS PER DAY
TIME TO REACH CERINIA: 6 MONTHS
No. OF PASSENGERS: 4–6
CUBIC METRES: 900
COLOUR SCHEMES
• CREAM
• YELLOW
• GREEN

EMERGENCY SHUTTLE – YES

SPECIAL! BAGGAGE ALLOWANCE 60 KILOS!

ONLY £10,500,000 + VAT

25

Speaking 2

Student B

On these pages you have some information about the space capsules available.

1 With your partner, decide what your priorities are, and use the form below to make notes. You have £10,000,000 to spend, but remember, you can also make your other passengers pay!

The Pyramid	The Bus	The Cube	The Sphere

2 Now ask your partner for any other information you would like on the space capsules. When you have all the information you need, decide wi your partner which space capsule is best for you.

5 The Northern Peaks Race

Warmer

Cover page 29.

1 You have to choose a team of four people for a sailing race. Which of t
following people would you definitely *not* choose?

a skipper   a navigator   a radio operator   a runner   a cyclist
a physiotherapist   a sailor   a cook   a weight-lifter   a sports trainer

2 Here is an article about a special race. Read the article and make any
necessary changes to your choices in **1**.

THE NORTHERN PEAKS RACE

Every year, the Northern Peaks Race starts from the picturesque harbour of Aberdovey, on the west coast of Wales. It isn't an ordinary sailing race. It's called the Northern Peaks, not only because the race takes place in the north, but because the race also includes cycling *to* and running *up* three of the highest peaks in Britain.

The first stop is Porthmadog, where the sailing crews rest and check the boats. This is when the real work starts for the rest of the team. They have to cycle to the foot of Snowdon (the highest peak in Wales), where they leave their bikes and start the hardest part of the race – a marathon run to the top of the mountain and down again. When they get back to their boats, they move on.

The next destination is the tourist port of Ravenglass. There the athletes cycle off to Scafell Pike (the highest peak in England), where they repeat their marathon run. Then they cycle back to their boats and it's off again, this time following the west coast up to Scotland and Fort William on the mouth of the Caledonian Canal.

They go up the canal to Fort Augustus on Loch Ness (famous for its monster!). Here the boats stop for the third time. The riders get on their bikes and cycle to Ben Nevis (the highest peak in Scotland *and* the British Isles), where they start their third run.

But the race doesn't end there! The athletes have to get back to their boats. Then the crews sail back down the west coast through the Irish Sea to the starting point at Aberdovey – and the best crew wins!

3 Now read the article again and mark the route on the map.

Student A Look at page 29.
Student B Turn to page 30.

Student A

You are the skipper of the Blue Daisy, and your partner is the trainer. You want to enter this year's Northern Peaks Race. This is no ordinary race – team spirit and co-operation are extremely important. So is the ability to substitute for another member of the team. (Last year, one of the sailors was ill and had to go to hospital. Fortunately, the cyclist was also an experienced sailor, so she was able to help you to sail the boat.)

1   You and your partner are going to choose four people for the race. Below is some information about eight possible team members. Your partner has some more information about the same people. Fill in the extra information and then together choose your team.

NAME	AGE	SEX	EXPERIENCE	CAN:				NOTES
				SWIM	SAIL	RUN	CYCLE	
M James		M		Yes			No	
T Griffiths		M	Local sailing races	Yes	Yes			Lots of experience of the area
N Jones	31		Second in last year's race (fastest cyclist)				Yes	
R Paterson	26			No	No		No	Excellent cook!
C Davies		F		Yes	No	No		Really enthusiastic
J Davenport	27		Round-the-world sailor, amateur marathon runner	Yes	Yes	Yes		
K Michaels	32		On winning team in last year's race (fastest runner)			Yes	Yes	
N Rodgers		F		Yes	Yes	No	No	Tells great jokes!

2   Now write down the names of the people you chose.

Sailor 1	
Sailor 2	
Sportsperson 1	
Sportsperson 2	

3   When you have decided, discuss your choice with the class. Why did you choose these four people for your team?

Speaking

Student B

You are the trainer for the Blue Daisy's sports team in this year's Northern Peaks Race. It is your job to look after the sportspeople on the team. Remember that the race lasts over a week. During that time, you will be living, eating, and sleeping on the boat, so morale is very important. Last year's race was a great success because the team were very friendly and you had a superb cook (one of the sailors) on board.

1 You and your partner are going to choose four people for the race. Below is some information about eight possible team members. Your partner has some more information about the same people. Fill in the extra information and then together choose your team.

NAME	AGE	SEX	EXPERIENCE	CAN:				NOTES
				SWIM	SAIL	RUN	CYCLE	
M James	42		On winning team in this race last year		Yes	No		Sensitive to criticism
T Griffiths	17					Yes	No	
N Jones		M		Yes	Yes	Yes		Big-headed - thinks too much of himself
R Paterson		M	Tenth in the London marathon this year			Yes		
C Davies	38		Ex-Olympic cyclist - retired from competitions				Yes	
J Davenport		F		Yes	Yes		No	Inconsistent perform - a bit of a loner
K Michaels		F		Yes	No			Can't stand M James
N Rodgers	20		Sailing instructor in local races	Yes	Yes			

2 Now write down the names of the people you chose.

Sailor 1	
Sailor 2	
Sportsperson 1	
Sportsperson 2	

3 When you have decided, discuss your choice with the class. Why did you choose these four people for your team?

6 Murder

> a husband   a business rival   a hired killer   money
>
> political power   as he got up to speak   in his bed
>
> a knife   at a public meeting   poison
>
> as he left his office   a gun   at night in his sleep
>
> in a deserted street   bankruptcy

1 Look at the words above and write them under the correct heading below.

Murderer	Motive	Weapon	Scene of the crime	Time of death

2 Now work in pairs. Use some of the words and phrases above to invent a murder story. Compare your story with others in the class.

Student A Turn to pages 32–3.
Student B Turn to pages 34–5.

Speaking

Student A

Mr Arnold, a rich and influential businessman, has been murdered. You and your partner together have enough information to find out who did it, when, how, where, and why.

1 With your partner, work out where, when, and how Mr Arnold died.

2 Now make a list of your suspects. Compare your list with your partner's.

FORM 378456SJ	WEYBRIDGE POLICE STATION

POLICE REPORT

It was obvious from the condition of
Mr Arnold's body that it had been moved.

ADDRESSES

Mr Gregory
Apartment B
23 Corn Lane
Buddlestown.

BUDDLESTOWN

Mr Arnold of Concord Enterprises was found murdered this morning in Buddlestown bus station. A business colleague told reporters that Mr Arnold had no enemies, but a close friend of the family said Mr Arnold had made at least one enemy, a certain Mr Prosser.

Three years ago Mr Prosser was forced into selling his family farm by Mr Arnold, who converted it into a shopping complex and multi-storey car park. Mr Prosser's father, who had never recovered from the loss of his family home, died earlier this week of a broken heart.

Police are still investigating the scene of the crime and urge members of the public to come forward.

Mr Arnold

Mrs Arnold

3 Now for the difficult part. Who did it? Use the space below to help you make your deductions.

Speaking

Student B

Mr Arnold, a rich and influential businessman, has been murdered. Yo•
and your partner together have enough information to find out who d•
it, when, how, where, and why.

1 With your partner, work out where, when, and how Mr Arnold died.

2 Now make a list of your suspects. Compare your list with your partner•

FORM 378456SJ	WEYBRIDGE POLICE STATION
	POLICE REPORT

<u>Findings</u>
The knife found in Mr Prosser's garden had
Mr Gregory's fingerprints on it.

ADDRESSES

Mr Prosser
23 Elm Grove
Buddlestown.

I'M GOING TO KILL YOU ARNOLD!

DON'T MAK• ME LAUGH• PROSSE•

the security guard went off duty at 11.00

BLOOD

Mr Gregory's car

| FORM 399947554PF | WEYBRIDGE POLICE STATION |
| | King's Road, Weybridge, Surrey |

PATHOLOGIST'S REPORT

Estimated time of death: 11.20

Mr Arnold

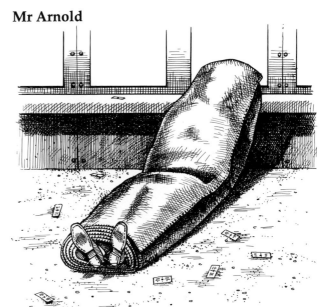

July 5 1992

Today Mr Arnold of Concord Enterprises married Miss Gregory, a former employee.

SUSPECTS DISAPPEAR!

Police are anxious to speak to Mrs Arnold and her brother, Mr Gregory, and Mr Prosser in connection with the crime. Anyone knowing of their whereabouts should contact the police immediately.

3 Now for the difficult part. Who did it? Use the space below to help you make your deductions.

Listening

Listen to a radio news broadcast about what actually happened. Then answer these questions:

1 Who did it?
2 What gave the murderer(s) away?

How green are you?

1 Match the words in A with their definitions in B.

A	B
1 green	a. care for the health and well-being of animals
2 to pollute	b. to treat used material so that it can be used again
3 the greenhouse effect	c. a form of oxygen
4 to recycle	d. the natural conditions e.g. land, air, and water, in which we live
5 extinct	e. not harmful to the environment
6 the environment	f. concerned about protecting the environment
7 environmentally friendly	g. no longer in existence
8 ozone	h. chlorofluorocarbons
9 animal welfare	i. to poison the air, water, or soil by adding harmful substances
10 CFCs	j. gradual warming of the earth's atmosphere

2 Now in pairs or small groups discuss the following questions:

– How concerned are you about the environment? Have you ever taken action as a result of your concern?
– Do you recycle things? If yes, what? If no, why not?
– What environmentally friendly products have you bought recently?

Now turn to page 38 and cover page 39.

Speaking 1   Cover page 39.

1   Read and answer the following questionnaire.

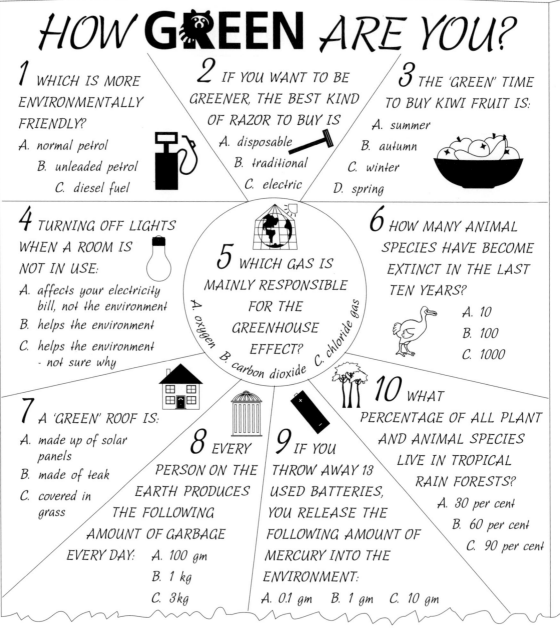

HOW GREEN ARE YOU?

1 WHICH IS MORE ENVIRONMENTALLY FRIENDLY?

A. normal petrol
B. unleaded petrol
C. diesel fuel

2 IF YOU WANT TO BE GREENER, THE BEST KIND OF RAZOR TO BUY IS

A. disposable
B. traditional
C. electric

3 THE 'GREEN' TIME TO BUY KIWI FRUIT IS:

A. summer
B. autumn
C. winter
D. spring

4 TURNING OFF LIGHTS WHEN A ROOM IS NOT IN USE:

A. affects your electricity bill, not the environment
B. helps the environment
C. helps the environment - not sure why

5 WHICH GAS IS MAINLY RESPONSIBLE FOR THE GREENHOUSE EFFECT?

A. oxygen   B. carbon dioxide   C. chloride gas

6 HOW MANY ANIMAL SPECIES HAVE BECOME EXTINCT IN THE LAST TEN YEARS?

A. 10
B. 100
C. 1000

7 A 'GREEN' ROOF IS:

A. made up of solar panels
B. made of teak
C. covered in grass

8 EVERY PERSON ON THE EARTH PRODUCES THE FOLLOWING AMOUNT OF GARBAGE EVERY DAY:

A. 100 gm
B. 1 kg
C. 3kg

9 IF YOU THROW AWAY 13 USED BATTERIES, YOU RELEASE THE FOLLOWING AMOUNT OF MERCURY INTO THE ENVIRONMENT:

A. 0.1 gm   B. 1 gm   C. 10 gm

10 WHAT PERCENTAGE OF ALL PLANT AND ANIMAL SPECIES LIVE IN TROPICAL RAIN FORESTS?

A. 30 per cent
B. 60 per cent
C. 90 per cent

2   Now discuss your answers with your partner.

Student A Look at page 39.
Student B Turn to page 40.

Speaking 2

Student A

How many questionnaire answers did you get right? Read the
information below and ask your partner for more information to check.

THE **GREEN** FACT FILE

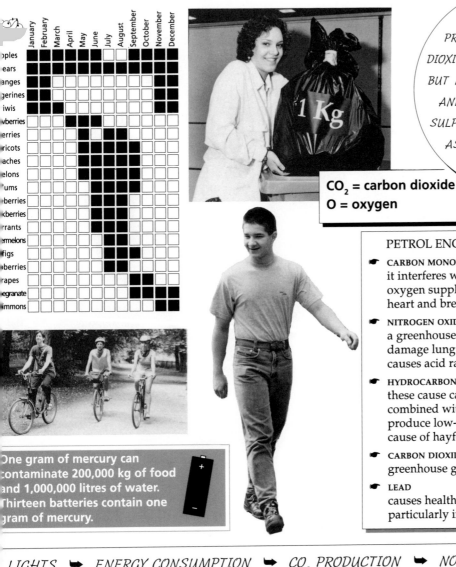

DIESEL ENGINES
PRODUCE LESS CARBON
DIOXIDE AND HYDROCARBONS,
BUT MORE NITROGEN OXIDES
AND ACID RAIN-CAUSING
SULPHUR DIOXIDE, AS WELL
AS HEALTH-DAMAGING
SOOTY SMOKE.

CO_2 = carbon dioxide
O = oxygen

PETROL ENGINES PRODUCE:

- **CARBON MONOXIDE**
  it interferes with the body's
  oxygen supply and aggravates
  heart and breathing problems

- **NITROGEN OXIDE**
  a greenhouse gas which can
  damage lung tissue and also
  causes acid rain

- **HYDROCARBONS**
  these cause cancer, acid rain and,
  combined with nitrogen oxides,
  produce low-level ozone, a major
  cause of hayfever-type allergies

- **CARBON DIOXIDE**
  greenhouse gas

- **LEAD**
  causes health problems,
  particularly in young children

One gram of mercury can
contaminate 200,000 kg of food
and 1,000,000 litres of water.
Thirteen batteries contain one
gram of mercury.

LIGHTS ➡ ENERGY CONSUMPTION ➡ CO_2 PRODUCTION ➡ NOT GOOD NEWS

GREEN PLANTS

O ⬅

Speaking 2

Student B
How many questionnaire answers did you get right? Read the
information below and ask your partner for more information to check.

THE **GREEN** FACT FILE

90%
*OF ALL LIVING
CREATURES LIVE
IN RAINFORESTS*

BUY FRUIT IN SEASON!
Fruit bought out of season has needed
fertilizers, energy in the form of lighting,
heating, and transportation. All of
these factors have a negative
effect on the environment.

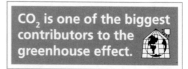

CO_2 is one of the biggest
contributors to the
greenhouse effect.

You can grow your own roo

CO_2 = carbon dioxide
O = oxygen

SPECIES EXTINCT

3000
2000
1000

1960 1965 1970 1975 1980 1985 1990

IN TERMS OF
PETROL CONSUMPTION,
PUBLIC TRANSPORT IS FIVE TIMES
MORE EFFICIENT THAN PRIVATE
TRANSPORT

*The production of every single object requires
energy. Energy means CO_2 production. It therefo
makes sense to buy objects that last, not objects
that are used once and thrown away. Objects su
as plastic cups, disposable razors, etc. create
rubbish that will last for the next 100 years.*

COMBUSTION OF WOOD, OIL, PETROL ➡ *CO_2 PRODUCTION*

The law

Farmer

1 Match the expressions with the pictures below.

1 Smoking in public places   4 Taking animals into restaurants
2 Dropping litter   5 Splashing pedestrians
3 Begging   6 Queue-jumping

2 In pairs or small groups, discuss the following questions:

– Are you allowed to smoke in public places in your country?
– Which countries do you think prohibit splashing pedestrians by law?
– For which of the above offences do you think people should pay a fine?

Student A Turn to pages 42–3.
Student B Turn to pages 44–5.

Speaking

Student A

Congratulations! You and your partner have just become joint rulers of Anygoway Island. You have been finding out what laws were passed by the last ruler.

1 Tell your partner about the four laws that were passed two years ago.

2 Listen to your partner telling you about the laws that were passed last year. Make notes on the form below.

Two years ago

Under Anygoway law, you are allowed to change one law for each of the past two years, and introduce two new laws for the current year.

3 Discuss with your partner which two laws (if any) you would like to change or abolish, and which laws you would like to introduce.

Laws to change or abolish

_____

_____

_____

_____

_____

_____

Laws to introduce

_____

_____

_____

_____

_____

_____

_____

_____

4 Finally, tell the other students about your new legislation. Would they like to live on your island?

Speaking

Student B

Congratulations! You and your partner have just become joint rulers of Anygoway Island. You have been finding out what laws were passed by the last ruler.

1 Listen to your partner telling you about four laws that were passed two years ago. Make notes on the form below.

2 Now tell your partner about the four laws that were passed last year.

Last year

Under Anygoway law, you are allowed to change one law for each of the past two years, and introduce two new laws for the current year.

3 Discuss with your partner which two laws (if any) you would like to change or abolish, and which laws you would like to introduce.

Laws to change or abolish

_____

_____

_____

_____

_____

_____

_____

Laws to introduce

_____

_____

_____

_____

_____

_____

_____

_____

4 Finally, tell the other students about your new legislation. Would they like to live on your island?

Warmer

John, Jack, and Jane went for job interviews yesterday.

─0 1 Look at the reported questions below and match them to the right person.

> I had an interview for a job as a security guard.

> I went for an interview for a job selling fruit and veg in a market.

> I was interviewed by two captains. I want to be a sailor.

JOHN   **JACK**   **JANE**

> They asked me if I had good eyesight.

> They asked me how much I weighed.

> They asked me if I could tie knots.

> They asked me if I suffered from seasickness.

> They asked me if I could swim.

> They asked me if I knew the difference between an old pineapple and a fresh one.

> They asked me if I was good at adding up.

> They asked me if I could speak loudly.

> They asked me if I knew how to use a gun.

2 Now work in pairs or small groups and discuss the following questions:

- At a job interview, what questions do you think a waiter/waitress or gardener would be asked?
- Have you ever had a job interview? What questions were you asked?

Patricia has just come out of an interview for a job. Listen to her telling another candidate about it. What job do you think the interview was for?

a doctor

a computer scientist

a model

a pilot

a biologist

a nurse

an optician

a shop assistant

Speaking

The interview game

This game can be played in pairs or groups. One player chooses a job from the list below, and imagines being interviewed for it. The other players try to guess what the job is, asking questions that start:

Did they ask you (if you) ... ?

The player who chose the job can only answer *yes* or *no*. You are allowe ten questions to guess the job. The player who guesses correctly chooses the next job.

accountant	farmer	police officer
actor/actress	firefighter	politician
architect	gardener	psychiatrist
artist	hairdresser	sailor
astronaut	ice-cream seller	tailor
baker	journalist	taxi driver
ballet dancer	lawyer	teacher
biologist	librarian	train driver
bus driver	musician	vet
clown	nun	waiter/waitress
cook	optician	window cleaner
doctor	pilot	
factory worker	plumber	

10 The old lighthouse

1 Match the words in A with their definitions in B.

A	B
1 lighthouse	a. a small building beside a river or lake for keeping boats in
2 beacon	b. a group of people employed to watch the coast, save lives, report passing ships, prevent smuggling, etc.
3 boat-house	c. a boat specially built to rescue people in danger at sea
4 lifeboat	d. a fire lit on a hilltop as a warning
5 coastguard	e. a tower or other structure containing a beacon light to warn or guide ships at sea

2 Work in pairs and answer the following question:
– Have you ever visited a lighthouse? If yes, describe it to your partner.
Now turn to page 50 and cover page 51.

Speaking 1

Cover page 51.

This old lighthouse is no longer in use and is now for sale. You and your partner have decided to buy it and turn it into a commercial business. You are interested in conserving its architecture and environment, and respecting its traditions. At the same time, the business must also make money.

1 Work in pairs. Look at the information below, and discuss how best to exploit the lighthouse. Make notes on the changes you would like to make.

The lighthouse was built in 1827, and its beacon was originally fuelled by paraffin. Six coastguards worked it, three at a time for a whole week. Each team was responsible for the lifeboats and the beacon. In recent years, only two coastguards looked after it, and they did not live in it - they checked the beacon by remote control from the comfort of the nearby coastguard headquarters.

The lighthouse was finally closed down on 31 December 1989. But it still remains standing, a familiar landmark which can be seen for miles along the coast.

2 Unfortunately, some people bought the lighthouse before you could buy it. You will now find out what they did to it.

Student A Look at page 51.
Student B Turn to page 52.

Speaking 2

Student A

1 Look at the plan of the original lighthouse. Then see how the new owners have converted it. Describe the changes to your partner.

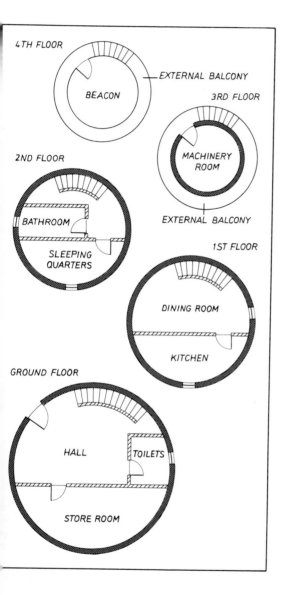

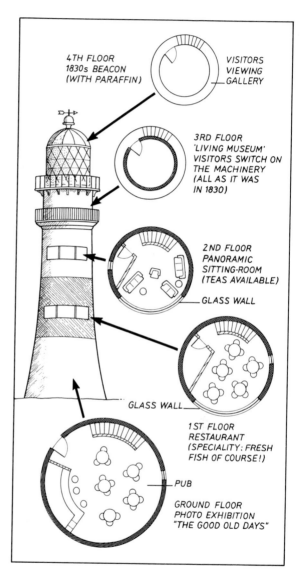

2 Now listen to your partner telling you about changes made to the exterior of the lighthouse and to the boathouse.

3 Do you like what the new owners have done? Why? Why not?

4 Now share your views with the rest of the class.

Speaking 2

Student B

1 Listen to your partner telling you about changes made to the interior of the lighthouse.

2 Now look at the plan of the original exterior of the lighthouse and the boathouse. Then see how the new owners have converted them. Describe the changes to your partner.

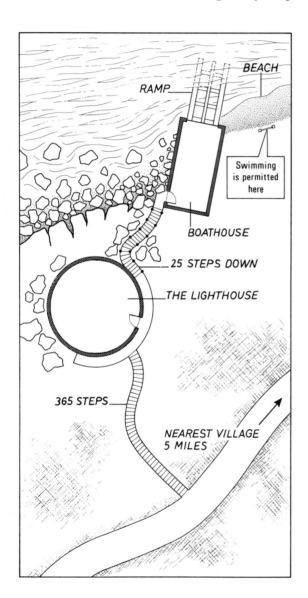

3 Do you like what the new owners have done? Why? Why not?

4 Now share your views with the rest of the class.

11 Recipes

1 Look at the words below and put them under the correct column heading.

| cake | pan | bake | chill | bowl |
| knife | cut | pour | oven | custard |

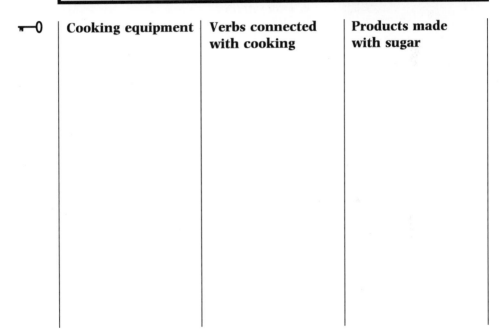

Cooking equipment	Verbs connected with cooking	Products made with sugar

2 Can you add another word to each list?

3 In pairs or small groups discuss these questions:

– Pizza is a favourite with the Italians. What food do you associate with the Chinese, the French, and the British?
– Are you a good cook?
– What's your speciality?

Now turn to page 54 and cover page 55.

Speaking 1

Cover page 55.

A culinary quiz
There are two parts to this quiz.

1 Look at the picture below. With your partner, answer the questions. If you don't know the answers, guess!

The Mystery Dish

1 Is it
  a. *sweet?*
  b. *savoury?*

2 What's it called?
  a. *Fruit surprise*
  b. *Trifle*
  c. *Yorkshire pudding*

3 What's in it?
  a. *milk, eggs, flour, olives, cheese, mashed potatoes, salt, pepper*
  b. *raspberries, custard, cake, cream, sherry, almonds, glacé cherries*
  c. *bananas, biscuits, custard, cream, brandy, oranges, coconut strips*

4 How do you cook it?
  a. *in the oven*
  b. *under the grill*
  c. *no cooking necessary*

5 How long does it take to make?
  a. *20 minutes*
  b. *30 minutes*
  c. *1 hour*

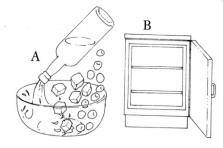
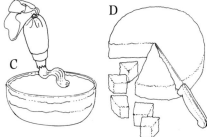
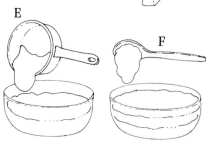

2 Now look at the various steps involved in making the mystery dish and try and put them in a logical order.

1 =   2 =   3 =   4 =   5 =   6 =

Student A Look at page 55.

Student B Turn to page 56.

Speaking 2

Student A

1 Look at the information below. Tell your partner the answers to the first part of the quiz. Then listen to your partner, who will tell you the answers to the second part of the quiz.

Old English Trifle

Serves 6-8   Preparation 30 mins

Ingredients

1 pint custard
1 Victoria Sandwich cake or 8 trifle sponges
175 g (6 oz) raspberries
100 ml (10 fl oz) double cream
40 g (11/2 oz) flaked almonds, toasted
50 g (2 oz) glacé cherries to decorate.

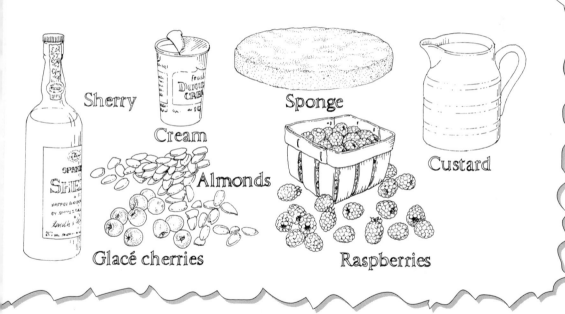

2 Now count the number of answers you guessed correctly and read the verdict!

> The verdict
> 9–11 What chefs!
> 4–8 Not bad for a first attempt!
> 0–3 Oh dear! Not born cooks!

Speaking 2

Student B

1 Look at the information below. Then listen to your partner, who will te
you the answers to the first part of the quiz. When he/she has finished,
tell your partner how to make the mystery dish.

The Mystery Dish

Sponge

Optional Chill before serving

2 Now count the number of answers you guessed correctly and read the
verdict!

The verdict
9–11 What chefs!
4–8 Not bad for a first attempt!
0–3 Oh dear! Not born cooks!

12 Treasure hunt

An eccentric millionaire has died leaving his heirs a complicated puzzle to solve before they can inherit his money.

1 Read the newspaper headlines and then write the information under the correct headings below.

A DIES AT THE AGE OF 92

ames Allbout, the eccentric millionaire, died at his amily home yesterday in the arms of his third wife, Elizabeth. Elizabeth is said to be heartbroken.

WILL CHILDREN CRACK SWISS BANK CODE?

J.A. DIES AGED 92

George ~ Alice

Bridget   James ~ Ann
~ Pat
~ Elizabeth

Catherine Christopher

CHILDREN TO INHERIT IF THEY CAN SOLVE PUZZLE

MILLIONAIRE FATHER LEAVES NOTHING BUT CLUES

SWISS BANKER SAYS NO NUMBER, NO MONEY!'

TWO SETS OF CLUES POINT TO ALLBOUT'S MILLIONS

Children must solve mystery of bank account number!

Name of millionaire	Names of children	Where the money is	How children can get the money

2 The two children have different sets of clues which they must share in order to get the bank account number. They have already found clue A. Can you see how they found it?

Dearest children
ill in the spaces correctly and the money is ours! Good luck!

) _____ (b) _____ by (c) _____ = _____
) _____ (e) _____ = _____

~ The Clues ~

) the fourth word of our _____?
) the day ...
) the age I started junior school
) an anagram
) september, February, the last two numbers of my phone number, the number of wives I have had, the day I became a millionaire

Now you need two letters (f). Put the letters between (g). Now put (h) at the end of the

Dearest children
Fill in the spaces correctly and the money is yours! Good luck!

(a) _____ (b) _____ by (c) _____ = _____
(d) _____ (e) _____ = _____

~ The Clues ~

a) _____ family motto
b) my best friend was born
c) plus one
d) U.P.S.L
e) 263901 - these are the numbers, but they're in the wrong order.

Now you need two letters (f). Put the letters between (g). Now put (h)

Go Forth & Multiply

Bridget

clue A

Student A Turn to pages 58–59.

Student B Turn to pages 60–61.

Speaking

Student A

This is the set of clues that James Allbout left Christopher. Your partner
has Catherine's clues. Look at the clues below and the information
opposite and work with your partner to solve the rest of the puzzle. If y•
get the number wrong, the money will automatically go to the Cosy Ca•
Retirement Home for cats!

Dearest children

Fill in the spaces correctly and the money is
yours! Good luck!

(a)_____ (b)_____ by (c)_____ = _____

(d)_____ (e)_____ = _____

~ The Clues ~

a) the fourth word of our _____?

b) the day ...

c) the age I started junior school

d) an anagram

e) September, February, the last two numbers
    of my phone number, the number of wives I
    have had, the day I became a millionaire

Now you need two letters (f). Put the letters
between (g). Now put (h) at the end of the
bank account number.

f) INITIALS

g) my lucky number and ...? (another number)

h) the seventh letter of my third wife's name

The account number: _____

JA DEATH TRAGEDY

Millionaire James Allbout (J A to his friends) died at his home in Oxfordshire yesterday. He was famous for his amazing business flair, his sense of humour and eccentricity. Now his love of puzzles has come back to haunt his children, Christopher, and Catherine. His huge fortune is safely tucked away in a Swiss bank. To get it, his children have to solve a puzzle!

Elizabeth, J A's third wife, said that as he grew older, J A had become increasingly eccentric. 'He was obsessed with cats and anything to do with the number 6,' she told our reporter yesterday. In spite of his eccentricities, J A will be much missed by all who knew him.

JANUARY

Bridget's birthday
Elizabeth's birthday

FEBRUARY

Harry's birthday!

MARCH

My birthday!

clue A

Go Forth & Multiply

Oxfordshire Times

6 March 1966 Edition no: 69662366

JA MAKES HIS TENTH MILLION

From: B C Allbout

UPTON SCHOOL
OXFORD
~♔~

JUNIOR SCHOOL
For boys aged seven to eleven

MIDDLE SCHOOL
For boys aged twelve to sixteen

Harry and Patricia

Harry
~ how about a game of tennis this afternoon? Phone me on 751960

JA

B I R T H   C E R T I F I C A T E
~ ♔ ~

Name: BRIDGET CATHERINE ALLBOUT

Speaking

Student B
This is the set of clues that James Allbout left Catherine. Your partner Christopher's clues. Look at the clues below and the information opposi and work with your partner to solve the rest of the puzzle. If you get th number wrong, the money will automatically go to the Cosy Cat Retirement Home for cats!

Dearest children
Fill in the spaces correctly and the money is yours! Good luck!

(a)_____ (b)_____ by (c)_____ = _____
(d)_____ (e)_____ = _____

~ The Clues ~

a) ____family motto
b) my best friend was born
c) plus one
d) UPSL
e) 263901 ~ these are the numbers, but they're in the wrong order.

Now you need two letters (f). Put the letters between (g). Now put (h) at the end of the bank account number.

f) my sister's ... but not A
g) something and nothing
h) the letter that comes before (alphabetically)

The account number: _____

JA DEATH TRAGEDY

Millionaire James Allbout (J A to his friends) died at his home in Oxfordshire yesterday. He was famous for his amazing business flair, his sense of humour and eccentricity. Now his love of puzzles has come back to haunt his children, Christopher, and Catherine. His huge fortune is safely tucked away in a Swiss bank. To get it, his children have to solve a puzzle!

Elizabeth, J A's third wife, said that as he grew older, J A had become increasingly eccentric. 'He was obsessed with cats and anything to do with the number 6,' she told our reporter yesterday. In spite of his eccentricities, J A will be much missed by all who knew him.

The Allbout family tree

George ~ Alice   Ronald ~ Flora

Bridget James ~ Ann Mary John

~ Patricia

Elizabeth

Catherine Christopher ~ Maria

Peter Helen

Go Forth & Multiply

clue A

THE DAILY MAIL

1 September 1936   Edition no: 19193666

J A 1 MILLION

Oxfordshire Times

6 March 1966   Edition no: 69662366

JA MAKES HIS TENTH MILLION

The Daily Telegraph

6 June 1966   Edition no: 666676

JA's SIXTEENTH MILLION

UPTON SCHOOL
OXFORD
~ ♛ ~

Name: *James Allbout*
Mark for effort: *A*   Mark for achievement: *B*

James has made good progress this year despite the difficulties he had at the beginning of the year.

Miss Vinegar

Bridget

Harry ~ how about a dinner party?

Don't forget! FEED THE CAT!

FEBRUARY   H's birthday party

MON	TUE	WED	THU	FRI	SAT	SUN
	1	2	3	4	⑤	6
7	8	9	10	11	12	13
14	15	16	17	18	19	20
21	22	23	24	25	26	

Listening

Christopher and Catherine are now in the Banque Suisse de Cerineuve talking to the Director of the bank. Unfortunately, there is a nasty surprise in store for them! In James Allbout's safe deposit box, there is nothing but a letter and a map.

Listen to their conversation and:

1 See if you got the bank account number correct.
2 Mark on the map where the money is.

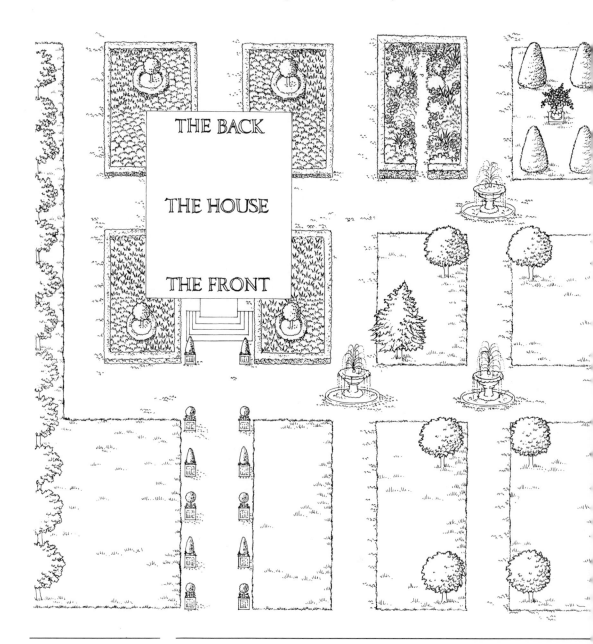

THE BACK

THE HOUSE

THE FRONT

Happy endings

Warmer

Discuss these questions in pairs.

- When did you last go to the cinema? What did you see?
- Do you prefer watching a film on TV or at the cinema? Why?
- Do you have a favourite kind of film or do you like all kinds of films?

Speaking

1 Look at the newspaper article below. It's about a revolutionary kind of film. Would you like to see a film like this?

NOW YOU TOO CAN BE A FILM DIRECTOR.

A new cinematic craze spreading across the United States like wildfire lets the audience write its own film scripts.

At each dramatic moment in the film the audience are given a choice. They can decide what the hero should do next: fight his enemies, kiss the woman of his dreams, and so on.

Simple control panels on each cinema seat give everyone in the cinema a chance to choose, and the majority decision wins and 'writes' the story of the film!

2 You and your partner are going to write a similar film. Working together, look at the opening shot of the film. Between you, you must decide what happens next. The options are given to you on the right. Discuss your choice and follow the numbers to the next shot.

Shot 1

Nick and Anna are coming home after a summer holiday in France. They are standing on the deck of the ferry. They don't know each other.

What happens next?
a She speaks to him (*go to Shot 2*).
b He speaks to her (*go to Shot 3*).

Shot 2

They have a drink together but then they are called to their cars and they part.

a They swap telephone numbers (*go to Shot 4*).
b They drive off in different directions (*go to Shot 5*).

Shot 5

Some months later they find they have both enrolled at the same business course and are sitting next to each other in the first meeting.

a He speaks to her (*go to Shot 10*).
b She speaks to him (*go to Shot 11*).

Shot 8

She accepts the invitation but suggests a foursome. She will bring her sister. He accepts and says he will bring his brother (*go to Shot 13*).

Shot 11

They get on quite well and she invites him to have lunch with her and some colleagues.

a He accepts (*go to Shot 15*).
b He says he's already got an appointment, but invites her to dinner (*go to Shot 8*).

Shot 14

He sends her flowers and a note to apologize. He asks if they can meet sometime.

a She invites him to lunch with her and some colleagues (*go to Shot 15*).
b She agrees and he invites her to dinner (*go to Shot 8*).

Shot 17

During the weekend it is obvious that Anna gets on very well with Nick's brother and that Nick gets on very well with Anna's sister.

a The four of them decide to go on holiday together (*go to Shot 21*).
b In fact, Nick asks Anna's sister to marry him (*go to Shot 22*).

Shot 3

She reacts coldly, answers his questions with monosyllables, and leaves as quickly as possible.

a He finds her name and number from the stewardess (*go to Shot 6*).
b He forgets about her and goes to his car (*go to Shot 7*).

Shot 6

When he gets back home he phones her and invites her out to dinner.

a She accepts (*go to Shot 12*).
b She suggest a foursome. She will bring her sister to the dinner and he will bring his brother (*go to Shot 13*).

Shot 9

He accepts the invitation.

a He arrives early with an enormous bouquet of flowers (*go to Shot 11*).
b He takes his younger brother with him for moral support (*go to Shot 29*).

Shot 12

The dinner is a great success. They decide to meet again. He invites her to his house in the country for the weekend (*go to Shot 16*).

Shot 15

The lunch is very interesting. It's obvious that she's a very important lady. They decide to do business together (*go to Shot 18*).

Shot 18

Anna is a very efficient and capable businesswoman. She works very hard and enjoys her job thoroughly.

a Nick loves working with her and their business is a great success (*go to Shot 27*).
b Nick knows that work is important but he also wants to have a private life (*go to Shot 26*).

Shot 20

He proposes to her and she accepts. They live happily ever after!

Now go to 3 at the bottom of the next page.

Shot 4

When they get back home

a He phones her and invites her out to dinner (*go to Shot 8*).
b She phones him and invites him to a party at her house (*go to Shot 9*).

Shot 7

As he drives off the ferry he is distracted because he's thinking about her and drives into the back of the car in front of him. It's her car!

a She is furious. They exchange insurance details (*go to Shot 14*).
b She takes it quite well, says there isn't any real damage, and drives on (*go to Shot 15*).

Shot 10

They get on well and find that they have a lot in common.

a He invites her to have dinner with him (*go to Shot 12*).
b She invites him to a party at her house that evening (*go to Shot 9*).

Shot 13

The dinner is a great success. The four of them get on very well and decide to go away to the country for a weekend together (*go to Shot 17*).

Shot 16

They have a wonderful time in the country and everything seems to be going very well. They start seeing each other more and more frequently.

a He is offered a new job (*go to Shot 19*).
b On the night of their first anniversary she prepares a special meal for him (*go to Shot 20*).

Shot 19

The job means leaving England and living in Japan for three years.

a She says she can't leave her job. It's too important for her (*go to Shot 24*).
b He asks her to come with him, to think about it and give him her answer that evening at dinner (*go to Shot 23*).

Shot 21

The holiday is a great success. The two couples fall in love. One night they make an important decision (*go to Shot 25*).

Shot 24

He thinks for a few moments and then

- says she is more important to him than the job (*go to Shot 20*).
- says that he can't give up his job for her and that she is being very selfish (*go to Shot 28*).

Shot 27

He prepares a surprise romantic dinner for her when she comes home from work one evening.

- She doesn't turn up until half past eleven. The dinner is ruined. Nick is furious (*go to Shot 28*).
- She is very impressed. They sit down to eat and then... (*go to Shot 20*).

Shot 22

When Anna and Nick's brother hear this, they are very happy.

- **a** A few months later, they too have some good news (*go to Shot 25*).
- **b** Nick's brother is offered a new job. It could affect their future together (*go to Shot 19*).

Shot 25

Both couples decide to get married on the same day and have a wonderful double wedding.

Now go to 3 at the bottom of the page.

Shot 28

He gets up, says, 'Right. I'm sorry, but I can't live with a woman who puts her job before me!' She replies, 'And I can't live with a selfish male chauvinist pig!' She gets up and walks out.

Now go to 3 at the bottom of the page.

Shot 29

Nick and Jo, and his brother, have a great time at the party. They meet a lot of great people. At the end of the evening, Jo invites Pip to dinner (*go to Shot 8*).

Shot 23

They have a romantic candlelit dinner for two.

- **a** She says she will leave her job and go to Japan with him (*go to Shot 20*).
- **b** She asks him to refuse his new job (*go to Shot 24*).

Shot 26

He invites Anna to his house for a romantic candlelit dinner together. He explains how he feels to her. He tells her that he loves her, but that if they are going to have a life together, she must be ready to work less and dedicate more time to their relationship.

- **a** Anna listens to him patiently, but then explains that she can't give up her job (*go to Shot 28*).
- **b** She agrees with him, and promises to devote more time to him and less to her work (*go to Shot 20*).

3 Now close your books and retell your story with your partner.

4 When everyone is ready, share your stories with the rest of the class and decide which one you like best.

Now turn to page 66.

Listening

The director watched the three endings and decided that he preferred the third, in Shot 28. But when he showed it to his producers, they said he had to have a happy ending, so he added five minutes to the end of the film. Here is the closing shot.

1   Work in pairs. Discuss these questions:

– How do you think Nick and Anna came to be here?
– How would you change the story to get to this ending?

2   Now listen to two people discussing the director's ending to the film. Is very different from yours?

T.13

Personally speaking

1 Work in pairs and discuss the following questions:

– What is your favourite time of day? Why?
– Which is your favourite day of the week? Why?
– Which is your favourite season of the year? Why?

2 Look at the adjectives below. Choose the two that you think best describe your partner.

artistic   sociable   hard-working

adventurous   laid-back   noisy

creative   quiet   intellectual

physically active

physically less active

3 Now tell your partner which adjectives you chose and why. Do you agree with your partner's choice?

You are now going to do a personality quiz.

Student A Turn to pages 68–9.
Student B Turn to pages 70–1.

Speaking

Student A

Below is the first part of a personality quiz. Your partner has the other half.

1 Explain the questions to your partner. Discuss and answer them, then fill in the answer grid for you and your partner on the page opposite.

Are you a
couch potato?

Answer this quiz to find out!

part 1

1 *When you go to the beach, what do you spend most time doing?*

   a. chatting and drinking at the bar
   b. reading a book in the shade
   c. playing volleyball
   d. swimming
   e. sunbathing

2 *Tick (✓) each activity that you or your partner have done.*

   a. Rock-climbing
   b. Run a marathon
   c. Competed in a team sport
   d. Visited more than five countries
   e. Published some original work

3 *How would you like to celebrate your birthday?*

   a. A candlelight dinner for two
   b. A night out at the local disco
   c. A night at the opera
   d. A special family meal at home

Are you a couch potato?
part 1

4 *Which animal would you prefer to be reincarnated as?*

a. a swan
b. a tortoise
c. a dolphin
d. a tiger

Write your answers here . . .

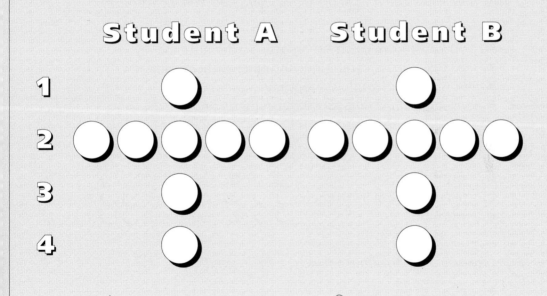

Student A   **Student B**

1

2

3

4

2 Now listen to your partner explaining the questions in Part 2, and answer them as before. This time your partner will keep a record of your answers.

3 Turn to page 72. Fill in your answers on the score sheet, and discusss the results.

Speaking

Student B
Below is the second part of a personality quiz. Your partner has the first half.

1 Listen to your partner explaining the questions in Part 1. Discuss and answer them together. Your partner will write down your answers.

Are you a

couch potato?

Answer this quiz to find out!

part 2

5 *When you take a day off work, what do you usually do?*

a. watch television
b. do housework/catch up on office work at home
c. go to concerts/exhibitions/the cinema/the theatre
d. go shopping/window shopping
e. go jogging/cycling/play tennis/other games

6 *Tick (✓) each activity that you or your partner can do.*

a. swim ◯ ◯ **b.** ski ◯ ◯
c. play a musical instrument ◯ ◯ **d.** paint ◯ ◯
e. windsurf ◯ ◯ **f.** hang-glide ◯ ◯

7 *If you won a million pounds, which would you do?*

a. put it in the bank
b. spend it on clothes
c. buy a fast car
d. go on an expedition up the Amazon
e. set up a fund for scientific research

Are you a
couch potato?
part 2

(8) *Which would you rather achieve or win?*

a. a Nobel Prize for physics
b. a Mr/Ms Universe award
c. publish a best-seller
d. an Olympic gold medal
e. a lot of money

Write your answers here . . .

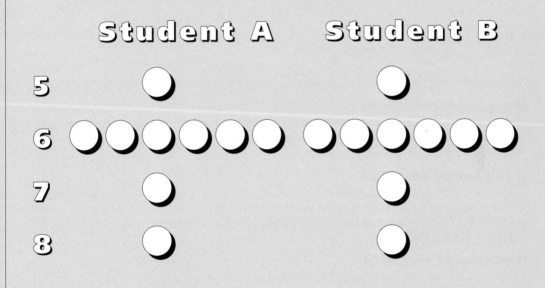

2 Explain the questions in Part 2 to your partner. Discuss and answer them, then fill in the answer grid for you and your partner in the spaces above.

3 Turn to page 72. Fill in your answers on the score sheet, and discuss the results.

Are you a
couch potato?
Score Sheet

Question 1
a. A   b. B   c. C   d. C   e. A

Student A ◯   Student B ◯

Question 2
a. C   b. C   c. C   d. C   e. B

Student A ◯◯◯◯◯

Student B ◯◯◯◯◯

Question 3
a. A   b. C   c. B   d. A

Student A ◯   Student B ◯

Question 4
a. B   b. A   c. C   d. C

Student A ◯   Student B ◯

Question 5
a. A   b. B   c. B   d. A   e. C

Student A ◯   Student B ◯

Question 6
a. B   b. C   c. B   d. B   e. B   f. C

Student A ◯◯◯◯◯◯

Student B ◯◯◯◯◯◯

Question 7
a. A   b. A   c. C   d. C   e. B

Student A ◯   Student B ◯

Question 8
a. B   b. A   c. B   d. C   e. A

Student A ◯   Student B ◯

Now read the comments on your characters. Do you agree with them? Why/why not?

If you scored mainly As . . .
You are an armchair adventurer - a true couch potato! You really believe in taking it easy, don't you? But sometimes it's fun to do something active, so give yourself a change - get off your comfy couch and get going!

If you scored mainly Bs . . .
You are a true intellectual - a budding genius, in fact. You love going to art galleries or the theatre. You probably do some kind of work which involves your creativity or your intellect. But be careful not to neglect your body. You know what they say: 'A healthy mind in a healthy body'!

If you scored mainly Cs . . .
You have adventure in your blood. You can't sit still for a second, and you aren't happy unless you're physically exhausted at the end of the day. You like to make the most of life, so sometimes it can be very tiring being in your company. Try to take things a little easier - relaxing can be fun too!

Tim and Jan are talking about their weekend. Listen to their conversation. How would they score on the test, do you think?

| **Tim** | Mostly As | Mostly Bs | Mostly Cs |
| **Jan** | Mostly As | Mostly Bs | Mostly Cs |

Tapescript section

Unit 1

1

I = Interviewer **SD** = Simon Davenport

I Hi, Simon, and welcome back. How was your trip?
SD It was great, really interesting. I'm glad I had the chance to go . . .
I How did it work out in the end? I mean, I remember you said before you left that you all had very different interests and very little time to do everything . . .
SD Yeah. I thought that might be a problem, but the organizers were wonderful – they planned activities to please everyone.
I And what was the highlight of the trip for you?
SD Well, let's see . . . I think the best thing, I mean the most interesting thing, was the visit to the local emergency services and the sports centre – they had a great sports centre – and it was really interesting to see how they do things over there.
I Great. Well, thanks Simon. And now, our next guest . . .

2

I = Interviewer **CS** = Catherine Smith

I Hi, Catherine, and welcome back. I hear the trip was a great success . . .
CS Oh yes, it was wonderful! I really had a good time. I met so many friendly people and it's a really great town, with so many things to do. You should go there sometime!
I I think I'll have to! So, what did you get up to?
CS Well, we did a lot of sightseeing, of course, and ate out in wonderful restaurants. The food was delicious, and I picked up a lot of tips.
I So we can look forward to some exotic new recipes at your bistro, then?
CS Yes, you certainly can!
I And what was the highlight of the trip for you?

CS Well, one evening I was invited to dinner at a local family's home and I was able to watch them prepar dinner and help out, too. That was a really interest experience. They were such lovely, friendly people .
I That's really great! Thanks for sharing that with us Catherine. And now let's turn to Jenny . . .

3

I = Interviewer **JW** = Jenny Wong

I Hello, Jenny. Well, was your trip a success?
JW Oh, yes, it was. I really enjoyed it. I mean, the organizers were great. They showed us exactly wha we wanted to see. I spent a day at a local high sch It's quite different from over here. I picked up a bit the language, too. But a lot of the young people the speak English really well. I was impressed!
I And what was the best part of the trip for you?
JW Erm . . . That's quite difficult to say, really. Let me . . . The last night, I suppose . . . We went out to th super restaurant and then to a local disco. I got to know a lot of people and we exchanged addresses. got a pile of letters to write!
I Thanks, Jenny. And now to our last guest . . .

4

I = Interviewer **PG** = Peter Grundy

I Good morning, Peter.
PG Good morning. I think almost everything's been sai about the trip. I'd just like to add a thank you on behalf of all of us to everybody who helped to orga the visit. We really enjoyed it a lot, and I can't wai go back.
I And what was the most interesting part of the trip you?
PG I met a local historian who's recording the local legends and traditions handed down from generatio generation. We discussed working together on a bo comparing the traditions and folklore of our two to It's amazing how much we had in common, really.

I look forward to reading that. Thank you very much, Peter, for being with us today. So that's all for now, folks. Don't forget to tune in on Tuesday for our next edition of *This could be your life*.

it 2

1 = Speaker 1 **Sp 2** = Speaker 2

1 And now back to the studio . . .
2 Late last night two burglars were arrested by a tree! The two men had stolen a van from outside a shop in the East End before breaking into a house in Ladbury Grove, in North London. The young couple who own the house were out celebrating a friend's birthday and came back to find their house had been broken into. Meanwhile, the thieves were already fifty miles away, speeding round a village green. The men didn't get away, however, as the van skidded on a bend and crashed into a tree on the edge of the green. When the police arrived at the scene of the accident, they recognized the stolen van and arrested the two men. They are being held at the local police station. So all's well that ends well. The young couple got all their belongings back. And the tree? Well, the local council have decided to put a rail up around it to protect it from future accidents.

it 6

Weybridge Crown Court jury finally arrived at a sion in the Arnold murder case today, after six hours of berations. They found Mrs Sarah Arnold and her ther, Mr Paul Gregory, guilty of murder in the first ree. Both were sentenced to thirty years' risonment.

Arnold, a rich businessman, had been stabbed to death his brother-in-law's apartment on the night of 6 June year, and had died instantly.

Court heard how Mrs Arnold (28) had married Mr old (55) for his money, and had then cold-bloodedly ted to murder him.

Arnold confided in her brother, Mr Gregory, who had eed to be her accomplice to the crime. The brother and er team tried to put the blame on Mr Prosser, who had ne time threatened to kill Mr Arnold.

They chose an evening when they knew Prosser would be alone at home with no alibi. Mr Gregory had invited his sister and brother-in-law to dinner. When Mr Arnold went to the bathroom, Mr Gregory was waiting for him and stabbed him in the back with a knife. Gregory then threw the knife out of the window of the flat into Prosser's garden, sure that the police would find it.

They then rolled Mr Arnold's body up in a carpet and carried him down to Mr Gregory's car. They drove to the bus station and left the body there still wrapped up in the carpet.

Initial police enquiries concentrated on Mr Prosser. All the evidence seemed to point to him as the murderer. But the brother and sister had forgotten one important detail – Gregory had left his fingerprints on the knife. This was the clue that finally led to the arrest and subsequent conviction of Mrs Arnold and her brother.

Unit 9

C = Caroline **P** = Patricia

C So how did it go, then?
P Quite well, I think. They were very friendly.
C What did they ask you?
P Well, you know, the usual things. How old I was, if I was married, which university I'd been to.
C Which one did you go to, by the way?
P Exeter University. They asked me what I'd studied, when I graduated, and . . .
C What did you study?
P I did a combined honours course in computer science and biology, and I graduated in 1992.
C Oh, really? That's interesting. I did medicine.
P And then they got more technical and asked me about eye complaints, problems, diseases, cures – that sort of thing.
C Did they ask you about the new laser treatment that can cure shortsightedness?
P Yes, they did, which was fortunate, because it's one of my pet subjects.
C Oh. That was lucky then . . . What else did they ask you?
P They asked me if I'd had any previous experience of this kind of job.
C What did you tell them?
P I said I'd worked for *Eyes Right* for a whole year. That seemed to impress them!

75

C Oh. When will they let us know who's got the job?

P They said they'd be letting everyone know by the end of next week.

C Oh, that's good. At least we won't have to wait too long . . .

Unit 12

BM = Bank manager **Ch** = Christopher **Ca** = Catherine

BM And the number of the account?

Ch 926 BA 071 D.

Ca No, no. It's 926 BC 071 D.

Ch That's what I said, isn't it? 926 BC 071 D.

Ca No, but it doesn't matter now.

BM Well, thank goodness for that. For a minute I thought all the money was going to the Cosy Cat Retirement Home for cats! Well, here we are. Here's the safety deposit box.

Ch Thank you.

Ca But there's nothing there!

Ch Yes, there is. Look! There's a letter.

Ca And a map.

Ch Oh, no!

Ca Oh, yes!

Ch Go on! Read it!

Ca Right. 'My dear Christopher and Catherine, by the time you get this letter, I'll be dead and gone.'

Ch Oh, dear!

Ca 'But it does mean that you've solved the first part of the puzzle. Congratulations! All the family jewels are actually at home.'

Ch At home, after all this time!

Ca 'Follow these instructions and you'll find what you're looking for. Go out of the front door and turn left. Walk down to the fountain and then turn left again. Take the turning on the right just before the Rose Garden. When you get to the next fountain, turn right. The money and the jewels are buried under the tree immediately on your left.'

Ch Only Dad could think of something like this!

Ca Yes. 'Have fun! Love, Dad.'

Ch A joker to the end!

Unit 13

J = Jill **K** = Kate

J Did you go to see that film last night, you know, *Ne Ending Love*?

K Yes, I did.

J Well, what was it like?

K OK, I suppose. I mean, not great, but . . .

J It's a love story isn't it?

K Yes, it's a modern love story about this important businesswoman. You know, she works in the city, wears designer suits, that type.

J Yeah . . .

K Yeah, well, she and this man meet on a ferry crossin and she's all cold and practically ignores him, but th a few months later they meet at a business conferen and they go to lunch, you know . . .

J And I suppose she's really successful and he isn't?

K No, it's not like that. They decide to work together a things go really well. But she's a real workaholic an never relaxes or spends any free time with him. She even goes to the office on Sundays. He isn't too hap about it. He wants to spend more time just being together.

J Hey, a real role reversal!

K Yeah, that's the idea. In fact, the night of their first anniversary – you know, a year since they first met the ferry – he cooks her a really special dinner and he's going to propose. He's bought the ring and everything. But she gets held up at work and arrives really late. The dinner's ruined and they have an enormous row. In the end she gets up and storms o

J And that's the end?

K No, it's strange . . . I mean it feels like it should be t end of the film. You know, an unconventional sad ending, but then they've tacked on another five minutes at the end.

J So, how does it finish?

K Well, they both go their own ways for a bit. He resig from the company and sets up his own business. Sh really successful, wins a prize as businesswoman of t year. But at the ceremony he's there with a really attractive woman and they seem to be really enjoyin themselves. She suddenly realizes she loves him and thinks that she's lost him . . .

J Yes?

But the woman is his sister, not his girlfriend. After the prize-giving, he goes up to congratulate her and introduces his sister. The expression on her face shows him that she still loves him. The sister leaves them alone, and they walk out towards the car park together. Suddenly, they both turn to each other and apologize. There's no need for further words . . .
That's it? That's the end?
They kiss in the rain . . . and I imagine live happily ever after!
What a silly ending! I don't think I'll be going to see it!

it 14

Jan **T** = Tim

Did you have a good weekend?
Yes, really great. I mean, the weather was terrific, wasn't it?
Yes, it was. Sal and I went for a really long bike ride, up to the woods and to that little lake – you know, the one where you can climb the trees and dive in.

T Wow! That's a long ride. How long did it take you?

J Oh, not long. Only about two and a half hours.

T *Only* two and a half hours? Rather you than me! Oh, and how did your tennis go?

J Not bad, really. I got through to the semi-finals and then I had to play against Martina Garrett.

T Oh, yes, I know. She's really good. Did she beat you in straight sets?

J No. As a matter of fact, I won.

T Oh, well done!

J I was really pleased. And what about you? How was your weekend?

T I had a relaxing time on the beach with a good book. That's my idea of fun!

J Uh huh. Hey, listen, it's Sal's birthday next Saturday and we're planning a beach barbeque. Would you like to come?

T Yes, I'd love to. But don't count on me for beach games!

J Well, we were thinking of using you as ref. for the volleyball tournament.

T Yeah, well I guess that's more my style!

Answer key

Unit 2	**What a night!**
Speaking	**1** a. 4 b. 8 c. 2 d. 5 e. 6 f. 3 g. 7 h. 1

Unit 7	**How green are you?**
Warmer	**1** 1f. 2i. 3j. 4b. 5g. 6d. 7e. 8c. 9a. 10h.

Unit 8	**The law**
Warmer	**1** 1e. 2f. 3a. 4b. 5c. 6d.

Unit 9	**Interviews**
Warmer	**1** They asked me if I had good eyesight. (John)
	They asked me if I was good at adding up. (Jack)
	They asked me if I could tie knots. (Jane)
	They asked me if I could speak loudly. (Jack)
	They asked me if I could swim. (Jane)
	They asked me how much I weighed. (John)
	They asked me if I knew how to use a gun. (John)
	They asked me if I knew the difference between an old pineapple and a fresh one. (Jack)
	They asked me if I suffered from seasickness. (Jane)
Listening	The interview was for a job as an optician.

Unit 10	**The old lighthouse**
Warmer	**1** 1e. 2d. 3a. 4c. 5b.

Unit 11	**Recipes**
Warmer	**1** Equipment: pan, bowl, knife, oven
	Verbs: bake, chill, cut, pour
	Products: cake, custard
Speaking	**2** 1 = D 2 = A 3 = E 4 = F 5 = C 6 = B

Treasure hunt

1   James Allbout's Swiss bank account number is 926 BC 071 D.

2   The money is under the tree marked X.

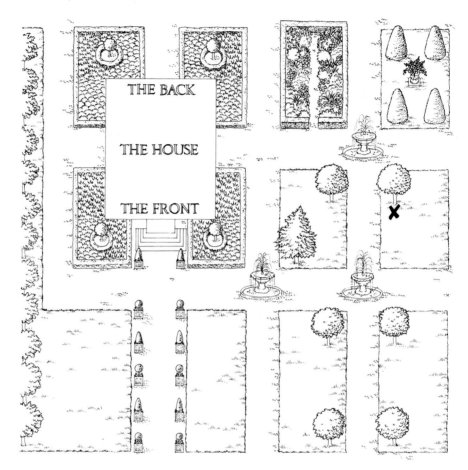